This book was made especially for:

MALIAH

Dear Maliah,

One can't imagine all the places you'll go and amazing things you'll do! Will you build new wonders? Discover new species? Swim in the deepest oceans?

Yes, great adventures lie ahead, and here are 250 words to describe them all. May your life be filled with wonder, magic, and all the good things in this book!

Love,

MALIAH *Goes* on a SAFARI

crocodile

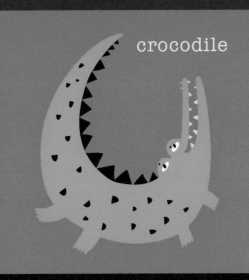

tortoise

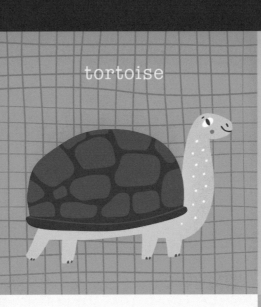

panther

flamingo

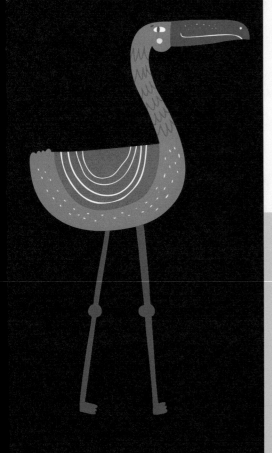

cheetah

gorilla

tiger

monkey

zebra

lion

elephant

gazelle

toucan

giraffe

warthog

hippopotamus

All Around
MALIAH'S HOUSE

phone

sofa

houseplant

table

chair

teapot

fan

mixer

sewing
machine

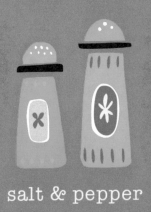
salt & pepper

clock

television

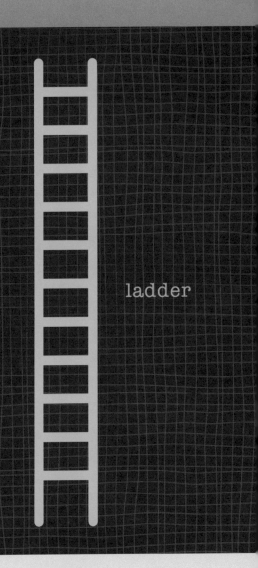
ladder

lamp

armchair

spatula

rolling pin

blender

Time to EAT, MALIAH!

peas

strawberries

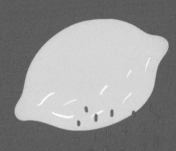

lemon

apples

radish

greens

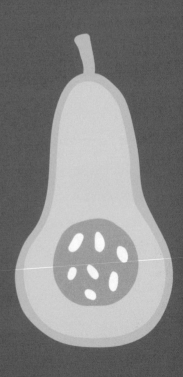

squash

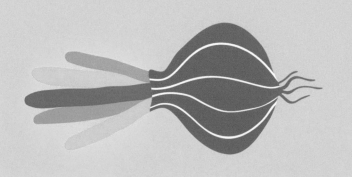 onion

 pear

 tomato

 broccoli

 pineapple

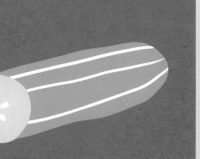 cucumber

 carrot

 banana

 pepper

MALIAH *Visits* the OCEAN

jellyfish

message in a bottle

seagull

lighthouse

fish

crab

sea shells

binoculars

anchor

waves

starfish

coral

seahorse

helm

whale

boat

MALIAH *Is* *on the* GO!

bus

car

fire truck

double-decker bus

garbage truck

roads

monster truck

convertible

truck

dump truck

airplane

tow truck

hot air balloon

ambulance

taxi

helicopter

ice cream truck

school bus

MALIAH *Goes* CAMPING

binoculars

canoe

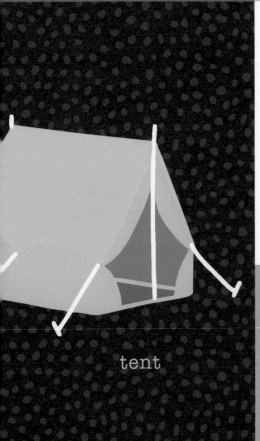

tent

camper

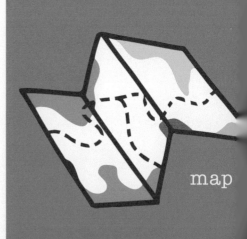

map

mountains

lantern

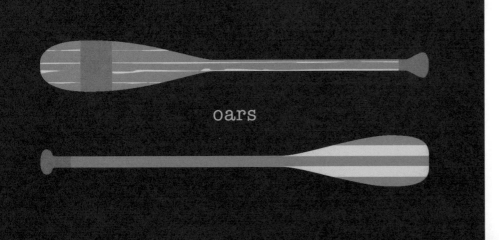

oars

camp chair

fire

compass

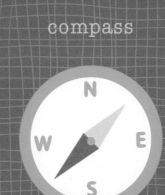

forest

backpack

boots

kayak

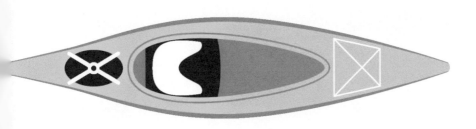

flashlight

What's OUTSIDE, MALIAH?

sun

puddle

thunderstorm

cloud

rain

snow

umbrella

thermometer

rainbow

snow shovel

winter

spring

tornado

summer

fall

wind

icicles

MALIAH *in the* GARDEN

basket

gloves

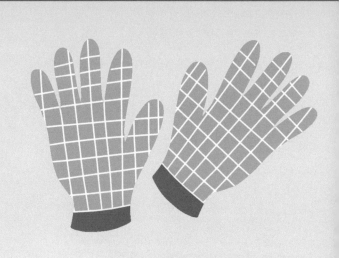

terrarium

pot

boots

hose

watering can

spray bottle

DINOSAURS Love MALIAH!

cave

Triceratops

Tyrannosaurus

Parasaurolophus

Stegosaurus

amber

jeep

hat

jungle

volcano

Pterodactyl

Diplodocus

Brontosaurus

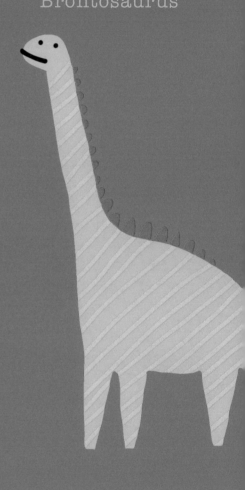

fossils

dinosaur eggs

footprints

Plesiosaurus

What Will
MALIAH BUILD?

caution sign

backhoe

front loader

dirt

house

forklift

bulldozer

steamroller

water
truck

cement mixer

safety
cones

crane

dump truck

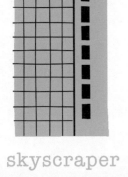

skyscraper

construction
workers

landscaping

MALIAH
in the CITY

park

subway

city
hall

streetlight

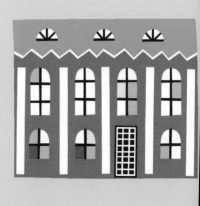

museum

bus

crosswalk

fountain

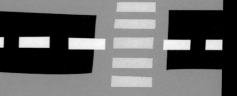

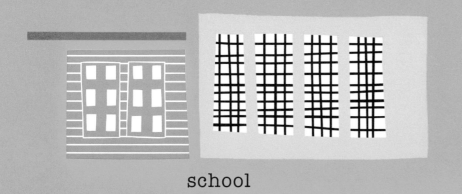

school

store

taxi

police car

apartment
building

food truck

traffic
light

railroad
tracks

bridge

MALIAH Visits the FARM

farmhouse

barn

haystack

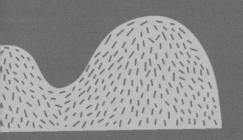

windmill

tractor

plate

cow

fields

chickens

dog

crops

chicken coop

sheep

fences

duck

orchard

pig

MALIAH'S *in a* FAIRYTALE!

ship

unicorn

magic potion

queen

king

fairy godmother

knight

jester

fox

crystal ball

castle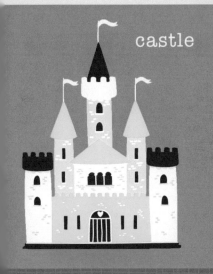

coach

dragon

key

cottage

mermaid

mushroom

BATH TIME

for MALIAH

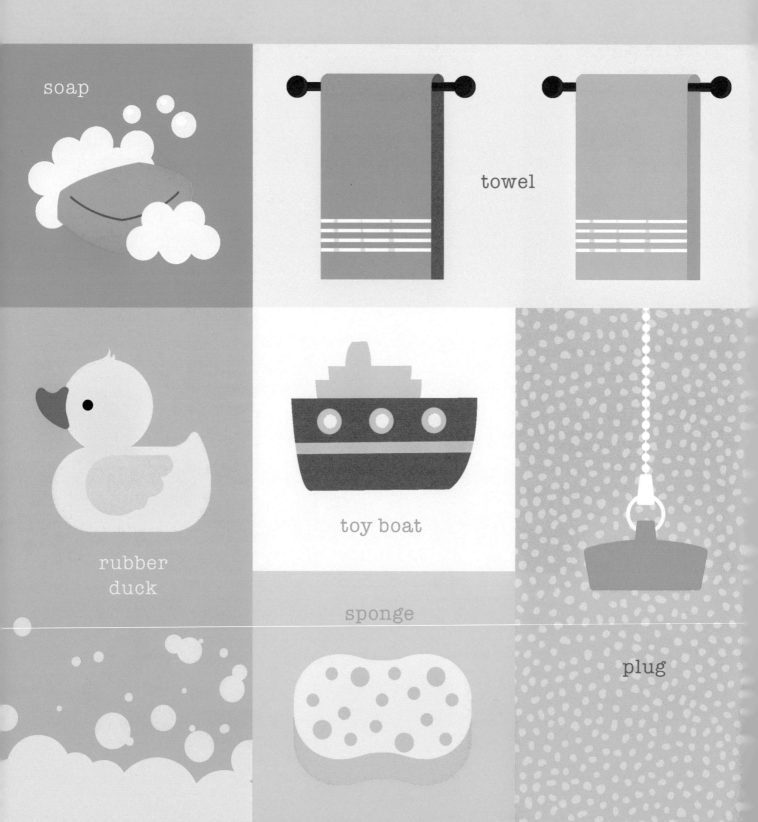

soap

towel

rubber
duck

toy boat

sponge

plug

faucet

bathtub

conditioner

shampoo

toilet paper

shower

bubbles

soapsuds

comb

SWEET DREAMS,
Dear MALIAH

pillow

moon

bedtime stories

dreams

floss

toothbrush

teddy bear

counting sheep

drink of water

bed

crib

night-light

basinet

bunk bed

constellation

stars

Cover and book design by David Miles

Artwork by the following talented Shutterstock artists: Beskova Ekaterina, Bukhavets Mikhail, Aleksandr Trusov, Sharon Silverman Boyd, KNST ART STUDIO, KateChe, tutti-frutti, Svetlana Kharchuk, GoodStudio, Angelina De Sol, katieromanoff_art, Didou, Nadzin, vectorchef, MirabellePrint, JeedChatt, nemlaza, lena_nikolaeva, Afanasia, ArtMari, IYIKON, metel_m, Alena Razumova, EgudinKa, kulyk, Alexander Ryabintsev, solmariart, Ruslana_Vasiukova, Inkley Studio, Incomible, Ira Bagira, Woodhouse, Andrii Bezvershenko, Follow Art, mckenna71, Ira Che, GoodStudio, tandaV, MG Drachal, Macrovector, Wondermilkycolor, Ksenia Zvezdina, Victor Z, momoforsale, vectortatu, Carboxylase, Kwirry, Buravleva stock, reddish, DoozyDo, Maike Hildebrandt, lyeyee, babystardesign, Kiarnight, Kataryna Lanskaya, Popmarleo, judilyn, Fresh Take Design, NotionPic, NadineVeresk, Sudowoodo, Angelina De Sol, twobears_art, Vector pro, lena_nikolaeva, Olga Zakharova, NadineVeresk, jsabirova, and PinkPueblo.

Made in the USA
Columbia, SC
08 November 2024